ENDANGERED ANIMALS AROUND THE WORLD

ENDANGERED AMPHIBIANS AROUND THE WORLD

BY LISA J. AMSTUTZ

PEBBLE
a capstone imprint

Published by Pebble, an imprint of Capstone
1710 Roe Crest Drive, North Mankato, Minnesota 56003
capstonepub.com

Copyright © 2025 by Capstone. All rights reserved. No part of this publication may be reproduced in whole or in part, or stored in a retrieval system, or transmitted in any form or by any means, electronic, mechanical, photocopying, recording, or otherwise, without written permission of the publisher.

Library of Congress Cataloging-in-Publication Data is available on the Library of Congress website.

ISBN: 9780756578350 (hardcover)
ISBN: 9780756578688 (paperback)
ISBN: 9780756578695 (ebook PDF)

Summary: From salamanders with lots of frills to squirmy creatures that look like worms, these endangered amphibians are having a tough time. Learn about some incredible amphibians that need our help to survive.

Editorial Credits
Editor: Ericka Smith; Designer: Sarah Bennett; Media Researcher: Svetlana Zhurkin; Production Specialist: Katy LaVigne

Image Credits
Alamy: Eyepix Group, 15, Nature Picture Library, 27, Xinhua/Song Wen, 22; Associated Press: File/Gerald Herbert, 11, Houston Chronicle/Johnny Hanson, 25; Getty Images: Billy Hustace, 23, Corbis, 9, izanbar, 12, Peter Finch, 5; John Measey: 18; Minden Pictures: Mark Moffett, 16; Shutterstock: Alfredo Maiquez, 17, asantosg, 7, Fliegenstube, cover, Francisco Gomez Sosa, 13, Jen Watson, 19, Rich Carey, 6, tristan tan, 21, Viacheslav Lopatin, 1, WhippoorwillGirl47, 29; U.S. Fish and Wildlife Service: 8, Robert Pos, 24

Any additional websites and resources referenced in this book are not maintained, authorized, or sponsored by Capstone. All product and company names are trademarks™ or registered® trademarks of their respective holders.

TABLE OF CONTENTS

All About Endangered Amphibians 4

Dusky Gopher Frog 8

Axolotl 12

Polkadot Poison Frog 16

Sagalla Caecilian 18

Chinese Giant Salamander 20

Making Progress 24

How You Can Help 28

    Glossary 30

    Read More 31

    Internet Sites 31

    Index 32

    About the Author 32

Words in **bold** are in the glossary.

All About Endangered Amphibians

What Is an Amphibian?

Splash! A frog hops into the water. It's home! Frogs are amphibians.

Amphibians spend part of their lives in water. And they spend part of their lives on land. Their name means "living a double life." Amphibians lay their eggs in wet places. Some are born with gills. They can breathe through their skin.

Some estimate there are about 8,100 **species** of amphibians. They include frogs, toads, newts, salamanders, and **caecilians**. Amphibians live on every continent except Antarctica.

What Is an Endangered Amphibian?

About one in three species of amphibians is **endangered**. That means there are very few of them alive. They are in danger of going **extinct**. They could disappear completely.

Why? Disease, pollution, **climate change**, and **habitat** loss make it hard for some amphibians to live.

Where Do Endangered Amphibians Live?

There are endangered amphibians all over the world. Many live in North America and South America.

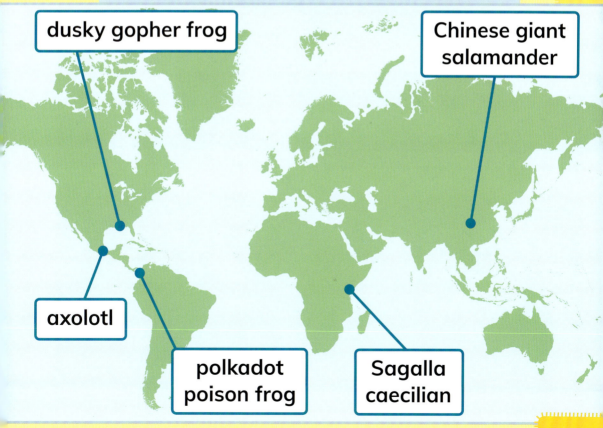

Here's where you can find the amphibians you'll learn about in this book!

Dusky Gopher Frog

Snoooooore. A dusky gopher frog calls for a mate. After **breeding**, he will go back to his **burrow**. It was made by a gopher tortoise.

Cutting down longleaf pine trees in Louisiana

Dusky gopher frogs were common in Louisiana, Alabama, and Mississippi. They lived in longleaf pine forests. But humans destroyed 99 percent of those forests. They cut the trees for lumber. And they built roads and towns. The gopher tortoises lost their habitat. So did the dusky gopher frogs.

In 2001, the dusky gopher frog became endangered. By 2009, there were only about 100 left. Now, they breed in just three small ponds in Mississippi.

Groups are working to save the frog. They are planting trees and protecting wetlands. Some zoos are raising dusky gopher frogs. They release tadpoles into ponds. With luck, some will survive.

Axolotl

Look at that "smile"! The axolotl is a salamander. But it does not live on land like other salamanders do. It spends its whole life underwater.

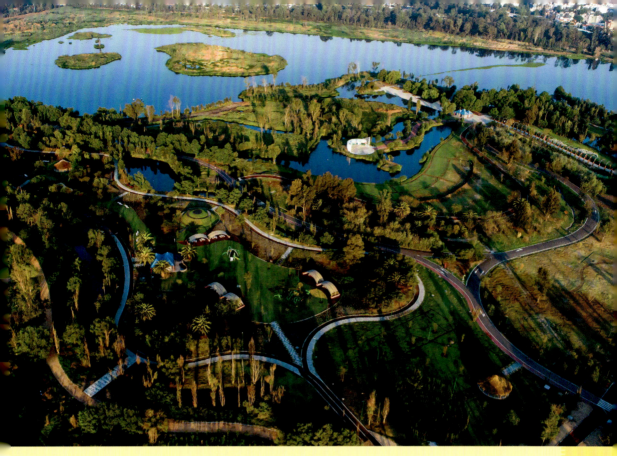

Axolotls live in Lake Xochimilco.

Axolotls are endangered in the wild. They once lived in lakes and wetlands of the Mexican Central Valley. Now they live in only one lake in Mexico City. In 2006, there were fewer than 250 in the wild.

Axolotls face many problems. Pollution makes the water quality poor. And invasive fish eat axolotls. People put the fish in the lake to use as food. But the fish harm other animals.

People are trying to help axolotls. Some people help clean the lake. Scientists help farmers build floating gardens in the lake. Axolotls can hide from predators in the plants' roots.

People clean the water where axolotls live.

Polkadot Poison Frog

Look at those spots! But don't touch. The polkadot poison frog's skin is **toxic** to humans.

This frog lives in Panama's **cloud forests**. But it is losing its habitat. People cut down the forests' trees. They build roads and farms.

A cloud forest in Panama

Disease is also a problem for the frogs. A fungus can kill them.

Groups are buying land to help cloud forest animals. Polkadot poison frogs live in these **reserves**.

Sagalla Caecilian

The Sagalla caecilian has no legs. It looks like a worm, but it's not! It's an amphibian. It lives underground on a few hills in Kenya. It needs soft, damp soil to live in.

Eucalyptus trees growing in Kenya

The Sagalla caecilian is endangered. **Erosion** has made the ground hard where it lives. In the 1950s, people began planting eucalyptus trees in the area. These trees dry out the soil too.

Now, people are planting **native** trees. The trees hold the soil in place. And they use little water. People are also removing eucalyptus trees to help the caecilians.

Chinese Giant Salamander

The Chinese giant salamander is the world's largest amphibian. It can grow up to 6 feet (1.8 meters) long! It was once found in many parts of China. Now, it is endangered.

Overhunting is a big threat. People kill the salamander for food.

Pollution and erosion harm its habitat too. The salamander cannot live in dirty water.

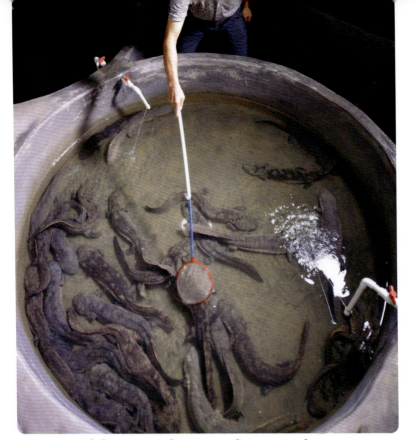

Chinese giant salamanders on a fish farm

Disease is also a problem. Some fish farms grow the salamander. The farmed salamanders are sometimes released in the wild. This can spread diseases to wild ones. The farms can also spread disease if people release the water they use without treating it.

People have made an effort to save the salamander. It is now illegal to hunt them. Groups have created 14 reserves to protect them. Still, the salamander is rare.

Making Progress

Houston Toad

The Houston toad of Texas has had it rough. It became endangered in 1970. By 2006, there were fewer than 250 in the wild.

To help, zoos started breeding the toad. Then they released the toadlets into the wild. But wildfires destroyed the area. The toad nearly went extinct.

A zookeeper takes care of Houston toads.

The zoos needed a new plan. They started putting eggs into ponds. They were protected by mesh. It worked! Slowly, the population grew.

Purple Frog

The purple frog of India lives underground. It comes out once a year to breed in mountain streams. But it's losing its habitat. People are cutting down forests. And they are polluting the streams.

The purple frog was listed as endangered in 2004. Scientists estimated there were only about 135 of them left at the time.

But there is hope. Volunteers are cleaning up waterways. They are teaching others to protect the frog too. Now the purple frog is doing better.

How You Can Help

Endangered amphibians face big problems. But small steps can make a difference. Here's how you can help:

» Ask your family not to use toxic chemicals at home. They can pollute waterways.

» Don't get wild amphibians as pets.

» Build a frog pond or toad house in your backyard.

» Spread the word!

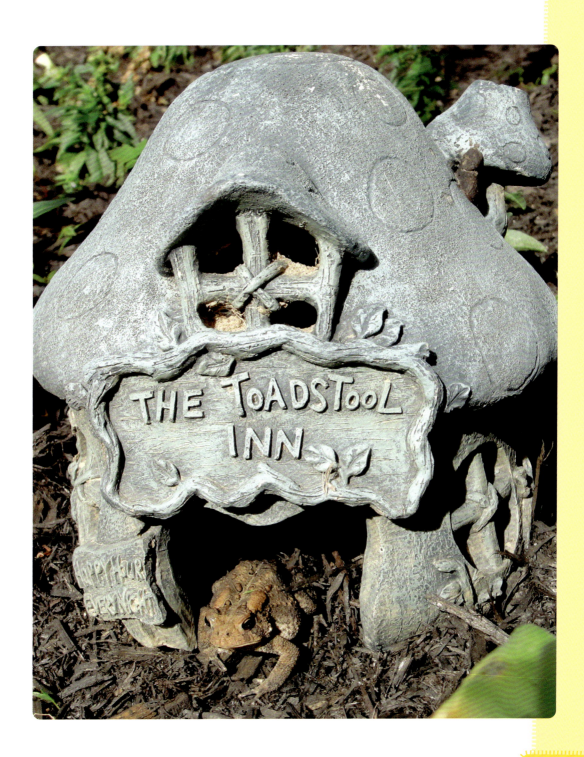

GLOSSARY

breed (BREED)—to mate and produce young

burrow (BUHR-oh)—a hole in the ground made or used by an animal

caecilian (si-SIL-yuhn)—a wormlike amphibian

climate change (KLY-muht CHAYNJ)—a significant change in Earth's climate over a period of time

cloud forest (KLOWD FOR-ist)—a thick forest with a lot of rain and low-level cloud cover

endangered (en-DAYN-juhrd)—in danger of dying out

erosion (ih-ROH-zhuhn)—when soil is worn away by water or wind

extinct (ek-STINGK)—no longer living

habitat (HAB-uh-tat)—the home of a plant or animal

native (NAY-tuhv)—growing naturally in a place

reserve (ri-ZURV)—land that is protected so that animals can live there safely

species (SPEE-sheez)—a group of animals with similar features

toxic (TOK-sik)—poisonous

READ MORE

Bodden, Valerie. *Frogs*. Mankato, MN: Creative Education and Creative Paperbacks, 2023.

Jaycox, Jaclyn. *Axolotls*. North Mankato, MN: Capstone, 2023.

Klepeis, Alicia. *Frogs*. Washington, DC: National Geographic Kids, 2023.

INTERNET SITES

Ducksters: Amphibians in Danger
ducksters.com/animals/amphibians_in_danger.php

Earth Rangers: What's So Great About Frogs?
earthrangers.com/EN/CA/omg_animals/whats-so-great-about-frogs

FrogWatch USA
frogwatch.fieldscope.org

INDEX

Alabama, 9
axolotls, 7, 12–15

burrows, 8

China, 20
Chinese giant salamanders, 7, 20–23
cloud forests, 16, 17

dusky gopher frogs, 7, 8–11

eucalyptus trees, 19

gopher tortoises, 8, 9

Houston toads, 24–25

India, 26

Kenya, 18, 19

Lake Xochimilco, 13

Louisiana, 9

Mexico City, 13
Mississippi, 9, 10

North America, 7

Panama, 16, 17
polkadot poison frogs, 7, 16–17

purple frogs, 26–27

reserves, 17, 23

Sagalla caecilians, 7, 18–19

South America, 7

Texas, 24

wildfires, 24

zoos, 10, 24, 25

ABOUT THE AUTHOR

Lisa J. Amstutz is the author of more than 150 children's books. A former outdoor educator, she holds degrees in biology and environmental science. Lisa enjoys learning fun facts about science and sharing them with kids. She lives on a small farm with her family.